A Writing Kind of Day

Poems for Young Poets

by Ralph Fletcher

Illustrations by April Ward

Wordsong
Honesdale, Pennsylvania

For Cynthia Rylant—your
delicious poems and stories
continue to inspire me.

—RF

Wordsong
An Imprint of Boyds Mills Press, Inc.
815 Church Street
Honesdale, Pennsylvania 18431
Printed in China

The Library of Congress has cataloged the hardcover edition of this book as follows:

Fletcher, Ralph.
A writing kind of day : poems for young poets / by Ralph Fletcher ;
illustrations by April Ward.—1st ed.
[32] p. : ill. ; cm.
ISBN: 978-1-59078-276-7 (hc) ISBN: 978-1-59078-353-5 (pb)
1. Children's poetry, American. I. Ward, April. II. Title.
811/.6 22 PS586.3F64 2005

First edition
First Boyds Mills Press paperback edition, 2005
The text of this book is set in 14-point Optima.

Illustration and Design by April M. Ward

20 19 18 17 16 15 14 13 12 11 10

Photograph credits: p. 13 SuperStock/Alamy; p. 30 image100/Alamy; Cover and p. 24
Comstock Images; p. 1 and 7 © 1995 by Jason Stemple, *Water Music*, Boyds Mills Press

Table of Contents

A Writing Kind of Day

It is raining today,
a writing kind of day.

Each word hits the page
like a drop in a puddle,
creating a tiny circle

of trembling feeling

that ripples out
and gathers strength
ringing toward the stars

Then it hit me!
Ma was my first word.
As if the word swam back
to where it all began.
So the word swam back
Then it hit me!

Writer's Notebook

My brother Tom says he's a hundredaire
with two hundred fifty dollars
in his bank account.

Dad's a thousandaire.
I gave baby Julia two pennies
so now she's a pennyaire.

When I look at Julia
her little bald head
reminds me of the planet Earth.

I put that in my writer's notebook
to maybe write a poem later on;
it feels like money in the bank.

Earth Head

My sister is three months old.
Her name is Julia
but I call her Earth Head.

She's bald on top
so on her North Pole
there's mostly Arctic tundra.

For all the most interesting parts—
eyes, nose, and mouth—
you have to look at the equator.

Memory Loss

It's not like losing a wallet,
or even your best friend.

Losing your memory is
losing yourself.

Each sentence Grandma speaks
makes me think of crossing a river.

She steps from word to word
until suddenly

she stops in the middle, disoriented.
Should she go back or keep going?

Mom takes Grandma by the hand
and helps her safely to the other side.

Poetry Recipe

Seems like my friend Xander
can write poems in his sleep,
good ones that win prizes.

I asked him how he does it
and he gave me his recipe
which I followed carefully:

two similes, one metaphor,
three unusual words,
and a dash of rhyme.

But my poem came out so bad
I felt like feeding it
to my Venus flytrap.

So I threw away his recipe
and tried one of my own,
a poem about my Grandma.

For my first ingredient I chose
her warped cutting board
that always smelled like garlic.

I wanted to add her wrinkly elbows
and the way she hums
while kneading her bread dough.

I picked up my best friend's pen
that I've kept in a drawer
ever since he moved away.

I took a deep breath,
opened my notebook,
and started to write.

Grandma

My Grandma loves to cook Italian:
manicotti, veal cutlet parmesan,
crusty bread like you've never had.

Over the years she's cut so much garlic
the smell is soaked forever
into her warped cutting board.

Now she's losing her memory.
But she still remembers
the summer I was three.

"You loved to play with the garden hose
but you kept turning around to say:
DON'T SHUT IT OFF, GRANDMA!"

She nods off while we're talking,
the skin on her hands so white
it could almost be made from clouds.

I slide a pillow behind her head,
wrap the old blue blanket around her,
whisper: Don't shut it off, Grandma.

now Angel

It's easy to make one,
lying on your back
in the newest snow.

You sweep your arms
up and down to make
a pattern that looks like wings.

Later you forget your creation,
go inside for some hot chocolate.
That's when she rises from the snow,

takes a feathery breath, tries her wings.
She skims over frozen lakes
like the faintest handwriting.

Later when you climb beneath the covers,
she peers in through your frosty window,
happy you called her into the world.

My Little Brother

My teacher says to use
metaphors and similes
whenever we write poems.

My brother Tom swoops in
like an F5 tornado
and destroys my bedroom.

He's a human wrecking ball
that crashes through my room
leaving trampled toys behind.

But I'd rather write it like this:
I've got an evil little brother.
And just
leave

it

at

that.

Writer's Block

We're doing grammar in school
which is bad enough but now
it's infiltrating my dreams.

I dreamed I was playing football
against a huge run-on sentence—
Coach said I had to stop him.

I threw a wicked block on that sentence
that knocked him into the next paragraph
and dislocated three compound words.

Verbs **cracked!** Nouns **splattered!**
That big sentence just splintered.
Til. Only. Fragments. Were. Left!

Bad Weather

They're predicting a big term paper
due to arrive on Monday morning.

Tuesday the forecast looks bad:
intense DOL and grammar drills.

Wednesday will be a scorcher
when the state writing test arrives.

Thursday there's a high probability
of five-paragraph essays.

Friday should bring some relief
when scattered poetry blows in.

Pinball

Stuck in a pinball game
(a.k.a. middle school),
rolling through halls,
binked and bonked,
smacked and spun,
whirled and twirled
by rules, teachers,
ideas, assignments.

When the game is over
the machine flashes

10 HIGHEST SCORERS

but you'll never find
my name on that list.

Bill of Sale

We read a poem
about a bill of sale
for a slave girl
named Lydia Wells.

She was sold for $133
on July 18, 1858, to a man
named Samuel Rothrock.

Coming home on the bus
I kept picturing Lydia,
the same age as me,
her bare feet in the dirt,
standing in the hot sun,
sold like an animal
to the highest bidder.

In a country like America
how could this ever happen?
How can I go on with my life?

Lost Poems

I wrote a bunch of poems,
stapled them together,
took them to a friend's house.

But they somehow slipped
through the floorboards
and disappeared.

I never got those poems back.
I tried to rewrite them
but they weren't the same.

One night two months later,
sleeping over my friend's house,
we heard restless sounds,

strange little noises
that my friend insisted
were nothing but squirrels or mice.

But I pictured my lost poems
scurrying on little feet
between the floors.

Beanstalk Poem

I had a happily-ever-after
fairy-tale kind of plan.
I would toss a few words
onto some empty paper
and grow a magic poem
mighty as a beanstalk
that I would climb
to fetch the golden
egg: an A+ grade.
I had it planned out
but I didn't figure
my teacher
would find out
I copied the poem
from someone else
and my beanstalk
would get cut down
and I'd come
crashing
down
with
it.

Hungry For Poetry

First of all I saw him chew
a tender Japanese haiku.

He ate a foot-long sonnet
with mustard spread upon it.

He downed a bag of ripe cinquains
while walking in the pouring rain.

He gulped an epic, chomped an ode,
wolfed a couplet to cure his cold.

He munched so many limericks,
they made him absolutely sick.

He tried a plate of fresh free verse;
but all that did was make things worse.

He took some onomatopoeia
to cure a case of diarrhea.

He ate a poem of sixteen lines,
and after that he felt just fine.

Venus Flytrap Rap

Venus Fly,
yeah that's my name,
munching houseflies,
that's my game.

I like moisture
and full sunlight;
distilled water
tastes all right.

But not as tasty
as a common fly;
I'll wait for days
'till one comes by.

Some call me
a carnivore;
in fact I'm an
insectivore.

I got green leaves,
got a little bitty flower,
but that's not where
I get my power.

All my traps
get set with care;
if a fly comes by
he'd best beware.

My fangs clang shut
like a prison cell,
and soon that fly
won't feel too well.

My enzymes
dissolve him slow,
'till a few more days
there ain't no mo'.

Venus Fly,
yeah that's my name;
munching houseflies,
that's my game.

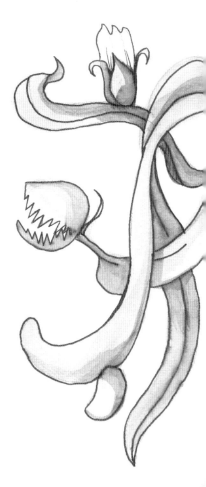

She Wrote Me a Love Poem

She wrote me a love poem:

Whenever you smile at me
I feel tiny hot air balloons
rising inside my heart.

It made me feel awesome
until a week later I found out

she gave the same exact poem
to a kid named Jamison Lee

so I guess my balloons popped.
It's like my cat Cleopatra

sweetly purring on my lap
like a symbol of world peace

until I go outside to find
the mouse she killed.

Squished Squirrel Poem

I wanted to write about
a squished squirrel
I saw on the road
near my house last week.

You can't write a poem
about a squished squirrel,
my teacher said to me.
I mean, you just can't do it.

Pick a sunrise or an eagle
or a dolphin, he suggested.
Pick something noble
to lift the human spirit.

I tried. I really did. But I kept
coming back to that squirrel.
Did his wife send him out
to fetch some food or something?

There was blood and guts
but here's what really got me:
he had pretty dark eyes
and they glistened still.

You can't write a poem
about a squished squirrel,
my teacher insisted,
but I don't think that's true.

Frost in the Woods

Uncle John lives in New Hampshire
near where Robert Frost was born.

He puts on his red plaid hunting shirt
and takes me hiking in the woods.

The leafless trees throw shadows
that dye the snow blue and black.

I ask him: Do you own these woods?
He answers: I'm renting them from God.

It's just the *tromp-tromp* of our boots
until my uncle stops to recite a poem:

> The way a crow
> Shook down on me
> The dust of snow
> From a hemlock tree . . .

When he's done the words keep echoing
in a quiet place that has opened inside me.

I ask him: Did you write that poem?
He says: I rented it from Robert Frost.

Metaphor

I was nervous about school
and our Poetry Unit test,
but first thing that morning
I got my brother dressed.

I found his Godzilla T-shirt
and pulled it over his head.
He pushed through his arms,
looked at them and said:

These are two smooth roads!

A metaphor! A nice one!
(Even though he's still a pest.)
And the weird thing is
he didn't study for the test.

Poetry

Poetry is like some
sugar-crazed teenager
who just got a license
but refuses to follow
the rules of the road.

It races out of control
then jams up the traffic by
going reeaaaaal slooooooow.
It turns up the music so loud
you can't sleep at night.
I can't figure out how it Decides
to capitalize certain Words.
Punctuation? Ha! A joke!
Won't use complete sentences.

And why does it refuse to
stay
on
the
line?

The most annoying thing?
Poetry won't shut up.
It embarrasses everyone
by telling the truth.

The Wordpecker

They eat words instead of insects.
A teacher captured one
and found the perfect job for him.

She gave him her kids' writing.
He could eat their misspellings
all day to his heart's content.

That was good enough for a snack.
But at night when the class was empty,
he sneaked over to the dictionary

to feast on big juicy words
like succulent and sassafras
and yum-yum-yum chrysanthemum!

Poetry Stands

They wanted to level
our favorite forest.

Our class sent the mayor
a swarm of angry verse;
we pelted the newspaper
with a blizzard of poems.

At my cousin's funeral
her family stood up
armed with nothing
but tears and poetry.

Poetry must wound
or heal those wounds.

When everyone else sits,
poetry stands.

Ma

Salmon hatch in a stream,
swim out to the ocean,

but they always return
to the stream of their birth.

Today I said: "Bye, Ma,"
and I got a funny feeling.

Then it hit me:
Ma was my first word.

As if the word swam back
to where it all began.

Poem Fossil

I had a strange dream:
a man dug up the bones
of a gigantic poem.

It was bloodthirsty, he explained,
with rhymes so ferocious
they could rip off your head!

Mighty poems once roamed
the valleys around here
but only their bones remain.

I woke with a sad feeling
until I remembered the truth—
poems are NOT extinct.

And I know it
                    because I'm a poet.

Bedroom Ocean

Dad says: Go to sleep,
but instead I lie in bed,
pretending . . .

The darkness is the ocean.
These fingers are seaweed
floating this way and that.

My oyster eyelids
slowly open and close.
My eyes shine like pearls.

A Writing Kind of Night

It is clear tonight,
a writing kind of night.

There's a moon stirring up
mysterious metaphors
in my imagination.

The heavens are jam-packed
with planets and black holes
that are still undiscovered,

and magnificent poems
that are still unwritten.